THUNDER,

SINGING SANDS,

AND

OTHER WONDERS

THUNDER, SINGING SANDS, AND OTHER WONDERS

Sound in the Atmosphere

KENNETH HEUER

FELLOW OF THE ROYAL ASTRONOMICAL SOCIETY

Illustrated with photographs and prints

DODD, MEAD & COMPANY New York

ENDPAPER. *Blizzard.* A pedestrian fights an intensely cold high wind filled with snow in Washington, D.C. Visibility has been greatly reduced by the storm. In this severe weather condition, the foot traveler is impressed by the sound of falling or blowing snow (Chapter 5).

FRONTISPIECE. *Lofty Tahoe pines.* The sugar pine of California is the largest of the trees of this class, often 200 to 220 feet tall and with a trunk diameter of 6 to 8 feet. Its crown is pyramidal, with horizontal or slightly drooping branches, and bears slender, bright-green needles 2 to 4 inches long and immense cones. In *Evangeline,* Longfellow writes of "the murmuring pines," an appropriate term for the coniferous forest shown here (Chapter 9).

1   2   3   4   5   6   7   8   9   10

Library of Congress Cataloging in Publication Data

Heuer, Kenneth.
    Thunder, singing sands, and other wonders.

    Bibliography: p.
    Includes index.
    Summary: Discusses the reasons behind certain
acoustical phenomena in nature, such as humming of
telegraph and telephone wires, murmurs of the forest,
and cracks of houses.
    1. Acoustic phenomena in nature—Juvenile literature.
[1. Acoustic phenomena in nature.   2. Sound]   I. Title.
QC809.A25H48   551.5   81–3312
ISBN 0–396–07973–3   AACR2

In memory of Brownie
who waits in a musical wood bordering the sea
and to Lotte
who remembers

Let me hear the clatter of hailstones on icebergs,
and not the dull tramp of these plodders,
plodding their dull way from their cradles to their graves.

HERMAN MELVILLE, White Jacket (1850)

Contents

Illustrations

THUNDER,
SINGING SANDS,
AND
OTHER WONDERS

Travels in the air. "Rain fell pattering on the balloon," writes James Glaisher, the English astronomer and meteorologist who made balloon ascents to obtain meteorological data in the nineteenth century. He heard this sound on June 26, 1863, almost 3 miles high—preferring it to the sound of heavy steps on earth! Who will listen to this weather noise in distant places, perhaps on other planets?

Foreword

In the open air, we are usually immersed in a sea of sounds, a number of which are caused by elements of the weather. Arousing the feeling of surprise, admiration, and awe, some of these acoustic phenomena are strange, unexpected, and incredible.

There is the familiar clapping and rumbling of thunder, which impresses one as being about the loudest of all noises. There is the wild howling of the wind, suggesting grief and sorrow to many. And there is the dull roaring of the avalanche, which alarms travelers in snow-covered mountains.

The study of sounds of meteorological origin is known as *atmospheric acoustics* (or *meteorological acoustics*). Meteorology is the science of the atmosphere and atmospheric phenomena, and acoustics is the branch of physics dealing with sound.

Atmospheric acoustics also encompasses the study of the role of the atmosphere in the propagation of sound. The atmosphere influences the transmission of these vibrations in many ways. Their velocity is, for example, governed by the temperature and molecular composition of the air. This aspect of the subject will not be treated here, but, after finishing the book, some readers may be inspired to investigate these meteorological effects on sound—another fascinating story.

The term *sound* means either a mechanical disturbance transmitted from one point in a material medium to another, which can produce the sensation of hearing, or the auditory sensation resulting from the disturbance. But meteorological acoustics is concerned primarily with the former of these meanings.

Sound is the general term for anything that is or may be heard. *Noise* usually refers to a sound that is unpleasant or disagreeable because it is too loud, harsh, or discordant. It may also mean a sound of any kind; the noise of the rain is often spoken of. *Tone* is generally applied to a sound regarded as pleasant or musical because it has regularity of vibration resulting in a constant pitch. Many meteorological sounds are not discordant but melodious. Indeed, as you will see, we are surrounded by weather music.

The meteorological sounds considered in this volume are arranged according to the weather elements causing them—atmospheric electricity, precipitation, temperature, wind, or a combination of such factors. In passing, the book provides an introduction to these things.

Some of the weather elements and the sounds they produce have been explained in traditional stories of unknown authorship, ostensibly with an historical basis. A number of these myths have been included, revealing the importance attached to the natural phenomena. Information has been provided on where and when the sounds can be heard. And some attention has been paid to the psychology of these noises—our emotional responses to them.

As a child, I wondered what produced the cheery cry of the snow as it was pressed onto the pavement by my boots. (I still love to hear this sound!) I wondered about the cracking of my grandfather's frame country house—the sudden, sharp noises that occurred so mysteriously on cold winter nights that I feared there were ghosts about. I wondered about the humming of telegraph wires. This singing was loudest when the temperature was low and a moderate breeze was blowing across the wires. No one could explain these marvels to me.

This book has been written for all those who, like myself, are delighted by and curious about such acoustic phenomena. To the best of my knowledge, this is the first work that has been written on meteorological sounds. But for it, the information on the subject remains scattered through scientific textbooks and journals that are not readily available. More or less apt descriptions of the phenomena are also to be found in the writings of poets, who have always been interested in them.

There are well-known weather noises, as the rattle of sleet, and those that may be unfamiliar to you, as the song of the sands. After reading *Thunder, Singing Sands, and Other Wonders,* you will have a greater chance of hearing the unusual sounds, because you will know what to listen for. And your understanding of the phenomena in general will provide greater enjoyment of them.

Keep your ears alert for these wonderful sounds in nature!

1

Clap and Rumble of Thunder and Musical Thunder

Thunder is one of the most familiar and probably the most terrifying of all meteorological sounds. The noise has been explained in many ridiculous ways—such as the bumping or rubbing of one cloud against another. If you observe carefully, however, you will soon see that it is preceded by a flash of *lightning*. Clearly, then, thunder is in some way caused by lightning.

Lightning is a visible electrical discharge associated with a *thunderstorm*. Some have suggested that thunder is due to the

Thundercloud. This is a common expression for *cumulonimbus*, a principal cloud type, exceptionally dense and vertically developed. The usual occurrence of lightning and thunder within or from it gives rise to its popular name. Appearing either as isolated clouds or as a line or wall of clouds with separated upper portions, they resemble mountains or huge towers. The upper portions are usually smooth, fibrous, or stratiated, and almost flattened, often spreading out in the shape of an anvil or vast plume. Under the base of cumulonimbus, which may be very dark, there are frequently low, ragged clouds, either merged with it or not. This towering mass of condensed vapor discharging a shower of rain was photographed from Brunswick, Georgia.

Thunderclouds photographed from space. The extraordinary view of thunderclouds over the Amazon Basin, Brazil, was made in March, 1969, on the Apollo 9 space flight.

mutual repulsion of electrons along the path of the discharge. Others have insisted that the sound is caused by the collapse of the partial vacuum produced by the heat generated by the lightning. Although plausible, these ideas are incorrect. The truth is that the electric discharge through the *lightning channel* causes a rapid heating of the air. A corresponding expansion of the gaseous matter at supersonic speed—simulating a violent explosion—also occurs along the path. This expansion, in turn, produces a compression wave in the surrounding atmosphere that travels outward exactly as would any other sound wave.

In a normal discharge (or *lightning flash*) to earth, a faintly luminous *leader stroke* is carried downward from a *thundercloud* in a series of steps. This initial stroke is frequently branched, the average number of downward-pointed branches being two or three. When it makes contact with the earth, it is succeeded with the much more luminous and rapid *return stroke* from earth to cloud, which retraces exactly the path taken by the leader stroke, including its branches.

A typical flash between cloud and ground is multiple. That is, the first stroke is followed in order by one or more others along the same channel. Each is begun by a downward, continuous stroke without the stepped structure of the initial leader and terminated by a return stroke. As many as 42 strokes have been observed during a single discharge, but two or three are more usual. They occur in such rapid sequence as not to be separated into component parts by the human eye but only sensed as a slight flickering of the discharge.

Because it transmits a more powerful flow of current, the return stroke of the lightning flash produces a much louder sound than the leader. The sound heard as thunder comes from the entire length of the channel and is modified by the intervening medium. The result is an impressive series of sounds that are variously described as *peals, claps, cracks, crashes, rolls,* and *rumbles.*

The part of thunder capable of being heard is deafening enough. But most of the sound energy lies in the range below the limit of hearing. This causes the familiar vibration of houses and the rattling of dishes and windows. It is because of this that Shakespeare writes in *King Lear*: "And thou, all-shaking thunder/Strike flat the thick rotundity of the world!"

The lightning channel is usually quite long and crooked, the thunder from the more distant portions arriving later than from the nearer. This accounts principally for its long duration. The

(ABOVE) *Cloud discharge.* The discharge of electricity may also be between two parts of the same cloud, as shown by this branching flash photographed in Westminister, Colorado. In this case, there is no return stroke, as far as is known—certainly nothing like the brilliant return sent up from the earth.

(LEFT) *Cloud-to-ground lightning discharges.* These discharges of atmospheric electricity between a cloud and the earth were observed at night in Boulder, Colorado. Note the downward-directed branches from the main lightning channels that give rise to the name *forked lightning.*

variations in the intensity of the thunder, which constitute its characteristic rumbling, are due first to the crookedness of the lightning channel, and second to the multiple nature of many lightning discharges and to echoing from mountains, hills, and other objects. As anyone who has heard it knows, the rumble of thunder is a low, heavy continuous sound like that made by heavy wagons.

At short distances of a few hundred yards from the flash, the thunder begins with a clap—a sudden, explosive noise made as by striking the hands together—followed by a long rumble. This is due to the fact that the nearest portion of the lightning's path gives the first and, normally, loudest sound. At increased distances, the thunder begins with a rumble.

Have you ever heard the thunder sing? On occasion, when the lightning is close by, the sound that follows begins with a *musical note.* It is caused by a series of lightning discharges, the kind that produce flickering, along the same path. When they occur at nearly equal time intervals, their successive thunder pulses blend into such a note. At any considerable distance from the lightning, the musical quality of the thunder is lost in the general rumble.

Light travels at 186,000 miles a second, and sound travels at about 1,100 feet a second. It is, therefore, possible to estimate the distance to the flash by measuring the time lag between it and the thunder and allowing 5 seconds for each mile (5,280 feet). For close lightning, the elapsed time until the beginning of the clap gives the minimum distance to the flash, and the time duration of the rumble is a minimum estimate of the channel length.

For example, if you hear a clap 2 seconds after you see the flash, the flash is at a distance of about 2,000 feet. If the clap is followed by a rumble of 20 seconds, the channel is at least 4 miles long. Because the conditions of the atmosphere during a thunderstorm are likely those least favorable to the far carry of sound, thunder is rarely heard at a distance greater than 15 miles.

Lightning occurs throughout the world. According to one estimate, 1,800 storms producing 100 flashes each second are in progress at any given moment. On a daily basis, there are 44,000 thunderstorms, which produce over 8,000,000 lightning flashes—and an immense number of claps and rumbles.

The frequency of occurrence of thunderstorms varies considerably with latitude and with the nature of the physical features of any region. Because high air temperatures and high humidities favor their formation, thunderstorms are more frequent in tropical and subtropical regions than in temperate latitudes. They occur on about 80 days or more a year in Florida, parts of South America, equatorial Africa, Madagascar, and parts of southeastern Asia. The most thundery part of the earth is the island of Java in the Malay Archipelago. There the annual number of days with thunderstorms is about 220!

The frequency is about 5 to 20 days a year in temperate regions. Because of the cold air near the ground and the stable conditions of the atmosphere, thunderstorms are scarce or nonexistent in cold regions (poleward of about 60° latitude).

As heating of the ground by the sun is often an important factor in their development, thunderstorms are generally much more common over the land than over the ocean. For the same reason, thunderstorms over land are more frequent in the afternoon than at other times of the day, and they occur more often in summer than in winter. But even in winter one may hear the voice of the thunder, which causes people to feel astonishment because it is unexpected.

Zeus. Found at Dodona, a center of worship of the earliest inhabitants of Greece, this small bronze of the wielder of the thunderbolt in the storms so frequent in that mountainous area exhibits great muscular strength. The statuette was probably made in the fifth century B.C. and is now in the Bayerische Antikensammlung, Munich, Germany.

2

Thunder and Lightning Gods

Since thunder accompanies lightning in storms, it is not surprising that they are often explained together in myths. Such natural phenomena were said to be due to the actions of superhuman beings.

In ancient Greece, thunder and lightning were manifestations of Zeus, chief of the Olympian gods. Any place struck by fire from the sky became sacred. If his thunder was heard on the right before battle, it was a foretoken of victory. The implication was that the enemy would hear it on the left, an unlucky sign. To the Romans also, Jupiter, god of the heavens, was apparent, if not invested with bodily nature and form, in thunder and lightning. In Rome, thunder on the left was auspicious; the sound occurring there at the beginning of any endeavor foretold success of the enterprise.

In Teutonic mythology, Thor was one of the greatest and oldest of the deities. He was god of peasants and common men, as opposed to Odin, who presided over the nobility. He was also god of thunder and brought the rains which were needed for the crops. His name was the Germanic word for "thunder."

Jupiter and Callisto. In 1613, Peter Paul Rubens, the great Flemish painter, signed and dated this work, in which Jupiter is symbolized by an eagle holding a thunderbolt between his claws. The Roman lord of heaven has assumed the guise of the goddess Diana (center) and is in conversation with the nymph Callisto. Diana's bow, quiver, and arrows are also visible. The painting is in the Staatliche Kunstsammlungen, Kassel, Germany.

Thursday is Thor's day, and no work was done on this day in North Germany and in many localities.

In order to guarantee success and favorable winds, the Normans, who called the god Thur, made sacrifices to him before a long sea voyage. The Saxons called him Thunaer, the Anglo-Saxons Thunar, and in most of Germany he was called Donar.

Thor is usually pictured as a tall, well-built, muscular man. He has red hair and a beard and, in the North, a halo of fire around his head. In his presence, the heat was so great that he was not permitted to use the rainbow as a bridge. As an alternative, he waded the rivers.

Thor possessed the marvelous hammer Miölnir, forged for him by the dwarfs. It represented the *thunderbolt*—an imaginary bolt, or elongated projectilelike mass, conceived of as the missile cast to earth in the lightning flash—and returned to his

Thor. This bronze statuette found in northern Iceland and dating from about A.D. 1000, depicts the deity with the wonderful hammer Miölnir on his knees. It is in the National Museum of Iceland, Reykjavík.

hand after being hurled. He had an iron glove, Iarn Greiper, which allowed him to handle his fiery hammer. His magic belt, Megingiörd, doubled his physical strength. He drove across the heavens in a brazen chariot drawn by two he-goats. The rolling chariot caused the rumble of thunder. Because it did not seem enough reason for the noise, in South Germany he was said to be carrying a collection of copper caldrons in his vehicle. This is how he got the impious name of kettle-vendor.

In China, thunder is sometimes represented as a superhuman being in shape and appearance much like a cock, having four claws to each foot and two hands proceeding from under the wings. In one hand he holds a chisel and in the other a mallet. A young goddess of lightning travels about with the thunder god to prevent him from making mistakes. Carrying a mirror in each hand, she flashes a bright light on every object in his path before he strikes it.

In Dahomey, West Africa, lightning is the element with which the thunder gods punish wrongdoers. Gbadě is the youngest member of this pantheon. Most easily angered, only he of the group of gods kills with jagged lightning. The eggs of crocodiles and lizards hatch because of his thunder.

A man killed by lightning is, as a consequence, convicted of a serious crime. His body is not buried by his family but is given to the priest and cult-members of the thunder pantheon to determine its fate. Cast away at the crossroads, his clothes are never touched again. If anyone should try to save something belonging to him, he also will be killed by lightning. The dead man's house is enclosed on all sides by an obstruction of palm fronds to keep people out.

During a thunderstorm in Dahomey, no one will mention the name of any god of the thunder pantheon. To do so would be to attract the gods' attention to himself.

Chinese deities of thunder and lightning. Good and virtuous people are never killed by thunder, according to the Chinese, but only those who have committed a breach of conduct, as in this popular image in which the thunder god is striking down a guilty person.

In the mythologies of nearly all North American Indian tribes, the phenomena of thunder and lightning are accounted for. Moreover, thunder is conceived as a person by many tribes, which tell stories of his deeds. These include tales of contests between Thunder and different personified forces of nature. The Kato Indians of California, as well as other tribes, even grant him the role of mankind's creator.

The supreme being of the neighboring Huchnom Indians is Taikomol. However, Thunder once challenged him. When he failed to do what Taikomol did—such as walking on the water —Taikomol sent Thunder north. In the spring Thunder was told he was to travel south and play with the hail, then return north in the winter.

In Coeur d'Alene Indian mythology, Thunder is a being who kidnaps a hunter's wife. He takes her to his cliff home, but the hunter follows the couple. When Thunder sleeps, the hunter steals his shirts, which provide Thunder with the power of flight. He is helpless without them, so he throws himself down heavily and weeps.

Thunder is an old man among several tribes in southern Oregon and northern California. His wife is an old woman or a tree. Thunder is a boy, according to the beliefs of other tribes in this region. Some say he is twin to a brother, Lightning.

Among the Cherokee, on the other side of the continent, it is also believed that the Thunders are two boys. They are Tame Boy and Wild Boy, often referred to as twins. They wear snakes as necklaces and bracelets and produce a thunderstorm when they play ball in the heavens. Powerful and beneficent, the boys are central figures in origin myths as well.

The concept of thunder as a large bird or birds seems to be very old and appears in different tribes of North American

Thunderbird. The powerful spirit in the form of a bird was often portrayed with an extra head on its abdomen, as in this wooden carving of the Kwakiutl Indians of Alert Bay, Canada. The figure is in the British Museum, London.

Indians and in Asia. This idea is found on the North Pacific coast, on the Plateau, and as far south as the Pomo in central California. It also appears among the tribes of the Plains and the Eastern Woodlands.

The Thunderbird or birds are powerful supernatural crea-

35

tures: they not only cause thunder but battle with various beings and forces and frequently grant divine blessings. The Crow Indians and other tribes depict them as wearing eagle cloaks. They produce thunder by flapping their wings. Lightning is brought about by opening and closing their eyes, or by ripping open trees with their claws in order to find a large grub to eat.

The association between thunder and birds exists in various South American tribes. But on the southern continent the Thunderbirds never received the same importance as in North America.

3

Sizzle of St. Elmo's Fire
and Swish of the Aurora

During stormy or threatening weather, a flamelike appearance is sometimes seen at prominent points on aircraft in flight, particularly at the tips of wings, and on land, at the tops of trees or steeples. In the era of sailing ships, it was often observed at the masthead and the yardarms. According to one report, on aircraft it takes the form of a fine brush of light or of a streamer a few inches to 15 feet in length and a few inches in width. Usually bluish or greenish in color, sometimes white or violet, the light is commonly accompanied by a *sizzling* or *crackling noise*. During daylight, it is hardly visible, but its sizzle can be heard in a quiet environment.

The phenomenon is called *St. Elmo's fire*, for the patron saint of Mediterranean sailors. This St. Elmo was the third-century St. Erasmus—Christian bishop, martyr, and also patron of sailors—whose name, Italianized as Ermo, became corrupted to Elmo. Another term for the flame-shaped light is *corposant* (holy body); early Mediterranean sailors believed it to be the

St. Elmo's fire on a ship at sea. In March, 1866, St. Elmo's fire appeared in stormy weather on an iron ship sailing in the English Channel. The captain distinctly saw a blade of light, not only at the extremity of the main-mast, but at the yardarms. The most vivid of these flames emerged from the bowsprit. Climbing to where it shot up into space, he approached his hand to the marvelous point (see illustration). The flame radiated no appreciable amount of heat, but, from the extremities of his fingers, the fire emerged and leaped into the air! The lights on the ship followed faithfully all the variations of the thunderstorm: each time that the wind increased, that the rain fell with greater fury, they were seen to increase in splendor.

St. Elmo's fire on a church steeple. The light has often been observed above the spire of Notre Dame, the noted Paris cathedral, during certain violent thunderstorms of a summer evening. Various observers of the phenomenon have reported a peculiar hissing sound, similar to the "singing" of water before ebullition, or a noise like that caused by the burning of wet powder, or one resembling the crackling of electric sparks.

actual presence of their guardian come to warn them.

Records of the occurrence of the phenomenon run back through many centuries and under different names. The ancient Greeks considered it a sign that their ship was under the protection of Castor and Pollux. These two youths were worshipped as the protectors of sailors, for Poseidon, god of the Mediterranean Sea, had given them power over winds and waves. Indeed, two of these lights appearing at the same time are often called *Castor and Pollux*. They signify that the ship will have good weather. One alone portends storm and is called *Castor*.

Pliny the Elder's *Natural History* describes the ghostly flame as appearing not only on masts and spars, but sometimes on men's heads. And in Julius Caesar's *Commentaries*, the Roman general and statesman says: "In the month of February, about the second watch of the night, there suddenly arose a thick cloud followed by a shower of hail; and the same night the points of the spears belonging to the Fifth Legion seemed to take fire."

Henry Wadsworth Longfellow, the nineteenth-century American poet, notes the phenomenon's weather significance in his narrative poem "Golden Legend":

Meeting of St. Erasmus and St. Maurice. In the sixteenth century, the German painter Matthias Grünewald executed one of his most luxurious works, the somewhat formal conference between St. Erasmus and St. Maurice. Erasmus is portrayed in bishop's robes and is accompanied by a bareheaded canon. Maurice was a Christian soldier of the third century, who, with his Egyptian comrades, was martyred. He is clad in silver armor, wears a headdress of pearls, and is followed by a dark-skinned archer. The great panel is in the Alte Pinakothek, Munich.

Last night I saw St. Elmo's stars,
　With their glittering lanterns all at play
On the tops of the masts and the tips of the spars,
　And I knew we should have foul weather today.

These apparitions behave just as mysteriously now as they did in the past. They have been observed whirling on a chimney top, seeming to jump down the flue at every lightning flash and then coming out again for another spin. In the deepest darkness, they have marked a boundary line, post by post, like lighted candles arranged in a row. On certain nights, people have been dismayed to see every steer in a crowded corral carrying lanterns on his horns. St. Elmo's fire may appear unexpectedly indoors, as well. A man sleeping in an attic reported he was awakened one stormy, terrifying night by light from sulphur-smelling candles on the footposts of his iron bed. But his agony was not prolonged. Soon a violent crash of thunder snuffed out the "devil's tapers."

Because they do not know the cause of the phenomenon, many people even now consider it to be supernatural and an omen of some kind. It is not the soul of a dead comrade with a message—good weather if the light rises, bad if it lowers—as superstitious German sailors believe. Rather, St. Elmo's fire is of the nature of a more or less continuous electrical discharge of a weak or moderate intensity in the atmosphere. Emanating from elevated objects at the earth's surface or from aircraft, the discharge occurs when the electrical field in the neighborhood of the object becomes very strong, as when a thundercloud is in the vicinity. The process by which an electrical conductor becomes electrified when near a charged body is known as induction. Aircraft may also develop a self-charge by colliding with ice crystals in clouds.

Spears of the Fifth Legion tipped with flame. During Caesar's African campaign, Castor and Pollux (for it is in this way that the Romans called the fire of St. Elmo) inspired the army with the confidence of victory.

The same phenomenon appears along certain power lines that carry high-potential currents. In this case, the glow is caused by the loss of electricity from the wire into the air. It is called a *corona discharge*, a term also applied to St. Elmo's fire.

Now, the visible electrical discharge consists essentially of innumerable tiny sparks. Each produces a correspondingly tiny "explosion" of the air through which it passes. As the discharge is fitful and of unequal strength, the result is a sizzling noise —a hissing sound, as of water about to boil. The sizzle of St. Elmo's fire is generally not heard more than a few feet away. However, occasionally the sparks grow larger and louder and frequently then end in, or with, a flash of lightning.

Another manifestation of atmospheric electricity is the *aurora*. Though most observers are impressed by the absolute silence of an auroral display, some have reported a *swishing sound*. The best place to listen for it is in high latitudes of both hemispheres.

The aurora is a luminous phenomenon of the upper atmosphere. In the Northern Hemisphere, this familiar and often beautiful sight, which occasionally is seen as far south as Mexico, is called the *aurora borealis*, or *northern lights*. In the Southern Hemisphere, it is called the *aurora australis*, or *southern lights*.

The aurora is frequently brilliant and assumes a variety of colors and shapes, including "draperies," "arcs," "rays," "bands," and "crowns." The lights may appear, change and disappear with great swiftness, though they may also remain constant for many minutes, or move slowly over the sky.

A variety of explanations are given by the peoples of northern countries for the aurora. In old chronicles, there are references to great fires burning at the distance, which probably were displays of these lights. Even in modern times, many fire departments have been called out at night because of them. The

Eskimos and Tlingit Indians believe the aurora is the spirits of the dead at play and occurs after the death of a large number of people. The Mandans say that it is an assembly of medicine men and warriors of northern nations boiling their prisoners and enemies in huge pots. The Norse explained it in terms of the light reflected from the shields of the Valkyries (battle maidens) while gathering the heroes slain in combat. And, in an Estonian folktale, it is said to be a wedding in the sky attended by guests whose sleighs and horses emit the radiance. Similarly, the aurora australis appears in the mythology of many southern lands.

Today it is known that the amazing auroral light is not sunlight reflected from polar snow and ice, as scientists once believed. Nor is it refracted light, like that of the rainbow. It is radiant energy emitted from definite regions of the upper atmosphere, but not, as in a flame, from a body of burning gas or vapor. It is more like the light of an electrical discharge.

The cause of the phenomenon is the collision of solar particles, guided and accelerated by the earth's magnetic field, with air molecules. More specifically, high-energy electrons and protons excite atmospheric atoms and molecules, which then emit characteristic radiation. Most of the light is given off by oxygen and nitrogen.

Many observers insist that they have heard the swish of the aurora as it swept past them. The term *swish* may be defined as a thin prolonged sound such as that produced by a whip rapidly cutting the air; also, a light sweeping or brushing sound as of a long or full silk skirt in motion. Other observers with years of polar experience state that they have never heard anything which they could attribute to the phenomenon. Finally, a few scientists say that they too have heard it but that it was something else. According to them, the swishes were timed in tune

with their own breathing and occurred only when the air temperature was extremely low. From these facts, they conclude that the aurora's swish is really the sound of one's own breath as its moisture freezes in very cold weather.

Instruments record no such sound during a bright aurora. There are, however, strong acoustic waves generated at frequencies below the limit of hearing. Perhaps that energy induces sound at times by a response, in the ear, that is not in a straight direction. It has been suggested that this might happen even in snow nearby. But no satisfactory explanation of the phenomenon has been given.

Who will solve this mystery?

Aurora borealis. This majestic spectacle was seen from Alaska. (Did the man with the camera hear the bands of light swish and crackle?) But, of course, the phenomenon is not all northern. Another photograph taken from the moon shows both polar auroras at once!

4

Patter of Rain

While thunder is likely the most frightening meteorological sound, the silver *patter of rain* heard during a shower is one of the most pleasing.

Any or all of the forms of water particles, whether solid or liquid, that fall from the atmosphere and reach the ground are called *precipitation*. Precipitation is produced as the result of the condensation of moisture in the air to form clouds. When some of the particles, by growth and aggregation, attain sufficient size, they fall out of the cloud to earth.

Rain is precipitation of liquid drops that have diameters greater than 0.02 inch. When the drops are smaller, they are usually called *drizzle*. Because as they increase in size they become unstable and break up, raindrops seldom have diameters larger than 0.16 inch. Concentrations of raindrops typically range from 3 to 30 for each cubic foot, whereas drizzle drops

Rain shower. A curtain of rain descends from a cloud over Grover, Colorado. Rapid changes in the appearance of the sky usually occur during such a summer storm.

are very much more numerous. The concentration of raindrops generally decreases as diameters increase. Except where rain is heavy, it does not reduce visibility as much as does drizzle.

Meteorologists classify the intensity of rainfall into four categories, depending on the hourly and six-minute rates of fall. Very light rain does not succeed in completely wetting an exposed surface; it is sometimes called a *trace*. The hourly rates corresponding to light, moderate, and heavy rain are, respectively: less than 0.10 inch, 0.11 to 0.30 inch, and over 0.30 inch.

A heavy rain of large drops makes a distinctive sort of patter, a quick succession of slight sounds. This patter is due to the successive falling of innumerable drops onto a body of water or any hard flat surface, such as a roof, paved street, or compact soil. An observer in a quiet environment may even hear an approaching shower for a considerable distance.

Precipitation from storms varies and so does the accompanying sound. Thunderstorms produce heavy rain and are usually of short duration. Rainfall in a thunderstorm at a particular place typically reaches peak intensity more quickly than it dies away. *Showers* are characterized by the suddenness with which they start and stop and by the rapid changes in force. Precipitation from *layer clouds,* clouds of no marked vertical development, is generally of lesser intensity and longer duration than that from shower clouds or thunderclouds and is usually composed of smaller particles. The amount of precipitation in a *cyclone* varies according to the velocity of travel of the disturbance. The slower the storm moves, the longer the winds blow into it at any given place and, therefore, the greater the duration and the amount of rain at that location. Very fast-moving cyclones may give but little or even no precipitation. Listen to the rain. Its patter is formed into compositions of definite structure and significance.

50

Splash of a drop. A raindrop strikes the earth's surface and is smashed by collision. The impact of these large drops makes a familiar weather noise.

Modern rain prints. Large raindrops have terminal speeds of about 30 feet a second and so may cause considerable compaction of the soil by their force of impact. These Colorado impressions are natural size. The rain fell on soft mud, which afterward hardened.

Ancient rain prints. Records of the precipitation of the past are found in the rocks, helping to piece out the story of prehistoric climates. These raindrop impressions on siltstone at Isle Royale, an island in Lake Superior, were made millions of years ago, before complex forms of life existed on earth. Rain fell silently in that remote geological age, if one's definition of sound requires ears to hear its patter! Compare these prints with similar ones in the photograph on page 52.

You are most likely to hear this weather noise in those parts of the world considered to be wet. The yearly rainfall averaged over the whole planet is about 30 inches, but this is distributed unevenly. The regions of highest rainfall are found in the equatorial zone and the *monsoon* area of Southeast Asia. Monsoon is a name for seasonal winds. In India, the term is popularly applied chiefly to the southwest monsoon and, by extension, to the rains which it brings. During the *rainy season*, there is heavy precipitation for one or more months. Middle latitudes get moderate amounts of precipitation, but little falls in the desert regions of the subtropics and around the poles.

The world's greatest average annual rainfall occurs in Waialeale, Hawaii. During a year, 460 inches of rain descend upon this mountain!

One of the compensations of being shut in by rain is the pleasure of listening to it. In addition to its peaceful patter and knowing that you have a roof against it, the sound is agreeable because the precipitation provides the principal source of fresh water for sustaining rivers, lakes, and all life on earth. Rain is therefore indispensable and overwhelmingly beneficial to man. It is made a god of, regarded with reverential respect, and associated with complex magical and religious ritual. This is particularly so in arid regions and those parts of the planet exposed to long dry seasons. The most important and influential member of a community is frequently the rainmaker.

In ancient Greece and Rome, the sky god—Zeus or Jupiter— was the god of rain. Greek rainmakers dipped a branch of his sacred tree, the oak, in water to induce precipitation, and the god was addressed with prayer. In Rome, small images were cast into the river Tiber to produce the descent of drops.

Rain was a blessing from heaven to the old Hebrews; it was given in return for obedience to the Law. In Genesis, the separation of the waters which were under the firmament from the "waters above" is mentioned, and the source of rain was conceived as a great reservoir or "treasure of waters" in heaven. The keys to these waters were kept by God; sin produced drought. Kings I relates the story of drought and famine in the land of Ahab, a king of Israel. It tells of God's promise to the prophet Elijah to send rain when the people's hearts were turned away from the false god Baal, the conversion of the people, the appearance of the little cloud, and the coming of the rain according to the promise.

Drought. In 1977, in eastern Colorado, want of precipitation results in wind-blown dust. When such a period of dry weather occurs, the patter of rain is a most welcome sound.

The Celtic druids went to certain sacred wells or magical springs. These priests of a pre-Christian religious order in Gaul and Britain were followed by processions. To make rain, they beat upon the surface of the water, or the water was poured over special stones, or it was tossed into the air.

Different animals are frequently regarded either as guardians of rain or as being under the care and protection of the rain god. These include frogs, toads, snakes, and lizards. To induce rainfall, they are humbly entreated, shown water, sprinkled, dipped, and submerged. If the precipitation is too heavy or continuous or floods threaten, the animals are laid by the fire until the earth is dry once more. Liberating rain by pouring water is a common magic practice. Pouring water on leaf-clad mummers or puppets, which symbolize vegetation, is still done in parts of Europe.

Rain is associated with thunder by many Indian tribes. In a Jicarilla Apache myth, Thunder and Cyclone questioned each other's powers and became angry with one another. As a result, there were no storms and no rains. Under the direction of four old men representing four water animals—Salamander, Water Frog, Crawfish, and Turtle—the Indians danced and concentrated on rain while Old Man Salamander sang. Water dropped from the clouds, and the ceremony is observed to this time by these Indians.

Whether thought of as a spirit riding a horse, as some Chaco Indian tribes do, or conceived of in other ways, the rain is viewed as doing good. Very heavy rainfall, of course, can cause great harm: soil erosion, landslides, and flooding.

5

Rattle of Sleet, Clatter of Hail, and Sizzle of Snow

Besides the gentle patter of rain, other sounds are produced by precipitation, as by *sleet*, generally transparent, globular ice pellets that have diameters of 0.2 inch or less. These icy particles form as the result of the freezing of raindrops or the refreezing of largely melted snowflakes. They may occur when a warm layer of air lies above a below-freezing one at the earth's surface.

The pellets usually bounce when hitting the hard ground and make a noise upon impact. The *rattle of sleet* on the windowpane is familiar to many people. Poets have sung about "iron sleet" and the rattle, or rapid succession of short, sharp sounds, produced by it. Frozen raindrops are sometimes driven along with considerable speed by the wind. At such times, if falling fast and the wind is subject to sudden outbursts, the ice pellets rattle irregularly on one's windows like separate handfuls of rice hurled at them.

When the ice particles have a diameter about 0.2 to 4 inches

Hailstorm over Colorado.
Hail occurs only in connection with a thunderstorm
and is produced by cumu-
lonimbus clouds. Stones of
at least walnut size fall 2
days or more a year in the
Denver area of Colorado.

or more, they are called *hail*. Thunderstorms which are characterized by strong updrafts, copious liquid water contents, large cloud-drop size, and great vertical height, are favorable to hail formation. Therefore, this form of precipitation often accompanies thunderstorms.

A single unit of hail is called a *hailstone*, which may be of any size from that of a pea up to that of a large orange or greater. The more severe a storm, the larger the stones produced. In September, 1970, ice pellets bigger than grapefruit battered the small Kansas town of Coffeyville. The storm generated the largest hailstone ever recorded in this century: it weighed 1.67 pounds and measured 17¼ inches in circumference! Because of its size, it must have fallen at a rate of nearly 100 miles an hour. In some instances, domestic animals on farms have been killed by blows from ice missiles of unusual size.

Hailstones may be spherical, conical, or generally irregular in shape. For the most part, the irregular ones seem to be clusters of smaller stones frozen together. The masses of ice that are shaped like a sphere are the most common. Typically, they have a layered interior structure like an onion. If you were to cut through the center of such a hailstone, it would show concentric layers of alternating clear and opaque ice.

According to the older theory of the formation of hailstones, the layered inner structure is explained by the rising and falling movements of the particle into alternate above- and below-freezing regions of the thundercloud. Some meteorologists, however, believe that descent alone from great heights through an updraft showing water-content stratification is probably enough to give rise to the characteristic structure. In either case, the hailstone grows basically by the freezing upon the ice particle of the supercooled water drops with which it collides. The nature of the ice depends upon such things as the rate of accretion, drop size, and temperature.

The *clatter of hail* is due to the fall of relatively large lumps of ice onto a roof or other hard surface. The series of light sharp clashes they make on a tin roof is considerable. So are the *crashes* they cause when falling on the glass cover of a greenhouse. The noises range further, from *thuds*, dull sounds, due to the impact of large hailstones on the ground to the combined *swish* of many stones falling simultaneously. The swish is occasionally reported in connection with severe storms. It is even said that hailstones are heard striking together in midair. It is unlikely that much noise is made by such collisions: the relative velocity of one stone against another is small as compared to the terminal speed of these objects when they strike the ground.

Hailstorms are commonest in the middle latitudes and usually last about fifteen minutes. They most frequently occur in middle to late afternoon. Listen for the sound produced by this type of precipitation then. If the stones are as big as baseballs and fall in quantity, they can raise quite a clatter.

Still another sound produced by precipitation is the *sizzle of snow*. Snow is composed of white or translucent ice crystals which drop from a cloud. These crystals are chiefly in complex branched hexagonal form and often clustered into *snowflakes*. When walking through the snow, you may see these snowflakes glow like pearls.

From earliest times, snow has attracted the attention and admiration of man. The Book of Job refers to the "treasures of the snow," thus hinting at its beauty. Snow crystals have exquisitely intricate shapes, but the symmetrical forms reproduced so many times in enlarged photographs of these tiny crystals are not found frequently in snowfalls. Much more typical are the

a

Anatomy of a hailstone. Shown here is the record-breaking hailstone that fell in Coffeyville, Kansas. The stone has an irregular shape; its projecting arms were made in the same way that *icicles* form (a). In a specially equipped "cold room" at the National Center for Atmospheric Research,

b

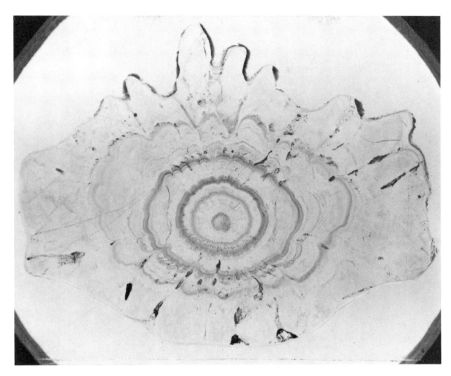

c

Boulder, Colorado, the lump of ice was cut in cross section for scientific study (b). It was revealed to be one single hailstone, displaying growth layers, roughly analogous to the rings of a tree (c). Polarized light shows the ice crystal patterns of the hailstone (d).

d

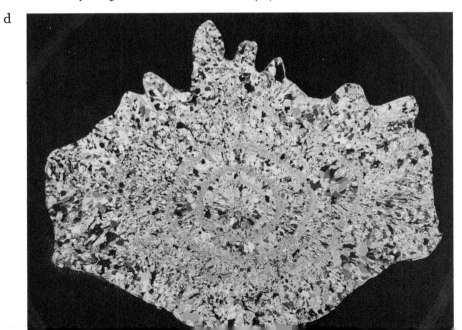

An aircraft damaged by hail. Heavy hail can batter a farmer's crop into ruins in a few minutes, dent automobiles and aircraft, and smash windows. In the United States, these ice pellets produce many millions of dollars of damage each year.

broken single crystals, fragments, or clusters of such elements.

Snowflakes made up of clusters of crystals or crystal fragments may grow as large as three to four inches in diameter. They often build themselves into hollow cones falling point downward. In extremely still air, ten-inch flakes have been recorded. People have actually seen them the size of dinner plates! Such is the "frolic architecture of the snow," as Emerson, the American poet, says.

When condensation occurs in the atmosphere at temperature well below 0°C (32°F), the usual result is small snow crystals. Larger snowflakes form at temperatures near the freezing point. In the absence of drifting or melting, snowfall is classed as slight, moderate, or heavy if the rate of accumulation is, respectively, less than 0.2 inch an hour, 0.2 to 1.5 inches an hour, or greater than 1.5 inches an hour.

The high-pitched silvery sizzle of snow is due to the falling or drifting of these ice crystals. The noise originates from the impact of the solid precipitation on the ground. The hissing is particularly audible in any heavy snowstorm accompanied by strong winds. The falling snow is not always silent, as some writers imply.

This aural phenomenon occurs to some degree on all continents, but in warmer climates it may be heard only in the extreme highlands where "ice stars" fall from the sky.

Song of the sleigh. In Arosa, in the Swiss Alps, a sleigh transports guests from the railway station to the hotel. When it is very cold, the ice crystals snap and break like glass under the runners, and the sleigh sings its loudest and best.

6

Creak of the Snow,
Report of the Snowquake,
and Roar of the Avalanche

If the *temperature* of the air and of the snow is sufficiently low, fallen snow does not melt but forms a cover on the ground. Nearly everyone who has experienced a cold winter is familiar with the *creak of the snow*. As it is pressed against a hard surface by a sleigh or automobile or even onto a pavement by the heels of one's boots, you can often hear its cheery cry. Children love to listen to this sound and never hesitate to ask a question that parents cannot answer: What makes the snow sing?

The white crystals are not always musical, not even when there is a large accumulation of them on the ground. When the temperature is just a little below the freezing point, the snow (then in a fine condition to form a ball) does not creak. And the wheel track is marked by a strip of more or less compact ice. In this case, the crystals of frozen water obviously melt, to a greater or lesser extent, as a result of the pressure to which they are subjected. They freeze together again as soon as the pressure is removed. The yielding is gentle and progressive through melting and flowing and not of that abrupt nature necessary to the production of sound.

On the other hand, when it is so cold that the snow will not form into a ball, it makes a prolonged sharp squeaking sound. The track left by the wheel is now marked by a trail of crushed and powdered crystals. In this case, the snow is too cold to melt under the pressure applied. Its yieldings and readjustments are abrupt and jerky, as a consequence of the crushing of the crystals and their slipping in a dry condition over each other. It is these abrupt yieldings, these sudden breaks and slips of its dry crystals, that produce the snow's creak.

An extensive area of snow-covered ground or ice, relatively smooth and uniform in appearance and composition, is known as a *snowfield*. This term is frequently used to describe such an area in otherwise coarse, mountainous, or glacial terrain. Another sound of meteorological origin may be produced there.

The earthquake is a well-known phenomenon, but who has heard of the *snowquake,* or *snow tremor*? This disturbance in a snowfield is caused by the simultaneous settling of a large area of thick surface layer. It occurs when wind action has maintained the top foot or more as closely packed, fine-grained snow, rather impervious to air movement. Meanwhile, at lower depths, old snow has been in the process of being transformed into ice. This process has caused the larger crystals to grow at the expense of smaller ones, creating air pockets and a weak structure. The collapse of the structure may be accompanied by a loud explosive noise—the *report of the snowquake*. The drop is discernible but rarely as much as 1 inch.

Over a large level field, adjacent patches may settle as a series of tremors. Now and then fine, powdery crystals may be blown upward through the crack of a settling patch. This is a *snow geyser*.

68

Avalanche. Huge masses of snow, mingled with ice, soil, boulders, and rubble roar down a mountainside above Zermatt, Switzerland, in January, 1954. The photograph gives a vivid impression of the horror of this manifestation of nature's destructive power.

Avalanche disaster. On February 13, 1951, at about 1 A.M., Airolo, Switzerland, was struck by a huge avalanche, moving on a front of 200 yards, with, in places, accumulations of snow 30 feet in height. People were buried and houses carried away. This street in the village was hit by only the smallest part of the fall.

When considered as a single particle, a snow crystal is at once beautiful or at least interesting in structural form and seemingly ineffective as an element of force or destruction. It is only when these crystals occur in nearly countless numbers that their presence causes concern or terror. This is true of many of the small things in nature.

At times snow may become so deep and unstable on a mountain slope as to form a terrifying *avalanche*, a mass of snow, perhaps containing ice and rocks, moving rapidly down the steep slope. The dull *roar of the avalanche* is commonly heard in mountains above the permanent *snow line.*

Some snow avalanches develop during heavy storms and slide while the snow is still falling. More frequently they occur after the crystals have piled up at a given site. When a mass of material overcomes frictional resistance of the sloping surface, an avalanche begins. This often happens after its foundation is loosened by spring rains or is rapidly melted by a warm, dry wind. Vibrations caused by loud noises—thunder, artillery fire, or man-made blasts—can start the mass in motion.

Avalanches may bring down thousands of tons of snow and can reach a speed of 200 miles an hour. In some older towns in Switzerland, a region of many mountains, buildings in open areas

The early-baroque church of Oberwald. This exposed house of worship in a village in the Swiss Alps is constructed in such a manner as to divert the flowing snow.

Anti-avalanche barrages. Protection against avalanches are given by these obstructions on mountains. Despite the construction of such barriers in Switzerland, overwhelming descents of snow still occur.

likely to be swept by avalanches are constructed like the prows of ships to turn aside the flowing mass.

The rush of wind produced in front of an avalanche of dry snow is called the *avalanche wind*. The most destructive form, the *avalanche blast,* occurs when the swiftly moving snow is stopped suddenly. This occurs in the case of an almost vertical fall into a valley floor. Such blasts may behave strangely, leveling one house without damaging its neighbor.

As the avalanche sweeps and grinds everything in its path, the loud, continuous, and confused sound heard by climbers, skiers, travelers, and residents of mountainous terrain may mean that death and destruction are on the way.

Blue Mountain Lake from the trail. Remarkable for fine scenery, the Adirondack Mountains in northeastern New York include numerous bodies of standing water. If you should visit one of the resorts for winter sports, you might hear the loud booming of a frozen lake.

7

Boom of Lakes, Burst of Trees, and Crack of Houses

Just as the roar of the avalanche is a feature of mountainous terrain, lake regions have their own distinctive sound.

Definitions that exactly distinguish *lakes, ponds, swamps,* and even *rivers* and other bodies of nonoceanic water are not well established. However, it can be said that lakes are bodies of slowly moving or standing water of considerable size that occupy inland basins. Ponds are small in comparison to lakes. *Marshes* and swamps contain large quantities of grasses, trees, or shrubs. And rivers and *streams* are relatively fast-moving. Lake basins have originated in many ways but mostly through *glaciation,* the erosion of rocks by passage of a glacier.

When the weather is cold, a loud *boom* is occasionally heard in lake regions. This uncanny sound is not the hollow roar of cannon. Rather, it is caused by the snapping and tearing of long rifts in thick ice—the result of a heavy strain brought on by the temperature contrasts, or in other ways.

Over much of the planet ice forms on lakes every year and

remains on these surface-water bodies for varying lengths of time. In some parts of the world, such as the Canadian plains, there is a seemingly endless skein of lakes covering the landscape. The state of Alaska has thousands of them. There is obviously a greater chance of hearing the boom of lakes in such regions.

The only place you are likely to hear the *burst of trees* is in a forest just after the beginning of an unusually cold period of weather. This sudden explosion is particularly startling to one alone at night in a thick growth of trees and underbrush covering a large tract of land.

Trees—those tall, woody plants that continue to grow each year and usually have a single main stem or trunk with branches that extend outward and upward at some distance above the ground—have been worshipped as gods, accepted as the dwelling places of good and evil spirits, and revered. These practices exist in some parts of the world today.

In Genesis, the Bible makes early reference to the tree of knowledge—the tree in the midst of the Garden of Eden whose fruit Adam and Eve tasted in spite of God's prohibition, thereby being driven from paradise. The name of the Druid priests of ancient Britain is derived from that of the oak tree they venerated. The use of holly, the leaves of *Ilex* trees, can be traced to the pre-Christian practice of the Druids. In winter, these natural philosophers who knew the courses of the stars, the size of the earth, and the properties of certain plants decorated altars with it.

In a sense, to enter a wood today is to confront one's past, to travel back through time to sacred trees and holy groves. Good and evil spirits still seem to lurk there, especially when the sun is beneath the horizon. If one hears the crack of a pistol

The Swett homestead. The cracking of this old frame house at Ground Nut Hill, Cape Neddick, Maine, must have caused the children who occupied it to get jumpy and fear the hobgoblins were about to get them. The team of oxen belonged to a farmer, and the sled was used to "break out the road" (much like a snowplow today). The photograph was taken in February, 1893.

where there is no pistol and none to fire it, it is no wonder that the timid are afraid. This unexpected noise is caused by the sudden splitting of the outer shell of some tree. The perennial plant has been strained beyond its strength by shrinking tighter and tighter under the chill of the frigid air about the relatively uncooled inner wood.

An apartment-reared generation is unfamiliar with the *crack of houses.* In order to hear this sound, you must live in an old frame house—a structure of which the form and support are made of timbers and which is sheathed with clapboards or shingles.

If you lie awake in such a dwelling in the country during the early hours of a calm and bitterly cold night, for example, you can listen to the snap, snap, bang of joists, rafters, and other parts as the stress of the cold jerks their joints into new adjustments. Every snap and bang comes unexpectedly and so mysteriously that little boys and girls think the house is haunted.

Modern families have been deprived of something worth hearing. The sounds a house makes have been replaced by those of the vacuum cleaner and dishwasher, the food processor and garbage disposer. A vain attempt to escape from these noises is made by turning up the TV or stereo. But an old frame building will tell you when winter is coming to an end. Spring is near when sounds become less brittle and more distant.

8

Howl and Whisper of the Wind and Hum of Wires

Other sounds of meteorological origin are any of the varied *aeolian sounds*, such as the *howling of the wind* over roofs and the *humming of telegraph wires*. These sounds are produced by wind when it encounters obstacles.

Aeolian pertains to the action or the effect of the wind. The word is derived from the name of the ruler of the floating island of Aeolia, Aeolus, to whom Zeus gave the control of the winds. In classical mythology, Aeolus' harp was held responsible for the murmur of the gentle breezes and his conch-shell trumpet was looked upon as the source of the gale's howl.

In the *Odyssey* of Homer, Aeolus gave Odysseus a favorable wind and a bag in which the unfavorable winds were confined. Odysseus' companions untied the bag; the winds escaped and drove them back to the island of Aeolia. Although human in the works of the great epic poet of Greece, Aeolus later became a minor god. In the *Aeneid* of the Roman poet Vergil, he was the god of the winds, which he kept shut up in a cave or released at the bidding of Jove.

Tower of the Winds. The tower was erected by Andronikos Kyrrhestes. Apparently it was a practical demonstration of scientific knowledge such as is seen today in public parks.

In Athens there is still standing an octagonal, marble building erected not later than 35 B.C. Called the Tower of the Winds, its eight sides face the points of the Athenian compass and carry a frieze of male personifications of the air in motion from these directions. The tower originally had a weather vane on the roof, though it was not a meteorological observatory. It was built to measure time, the walls bearing sundials, with a water clock made for use during cloudy weather.

Lambs were sacrificed by commanders of expeditions anxious for winds to assist their fleets. Boreas, the north wind, was especially honored by the Athenians for his part in the destruction of Xerxes' ships in 480 B.C. In mythology, he was the son of Aeolus or of Astraeus and Eos, the starry night and the dawn. Being cold and stormy, Boreas is represented on the Tower of the Winds by a warmly clad old man carrying a conch shell (probably to portray the howling of the wind).

In specific tales which have to do with regulating it, wind appears as a character in the mythologies of many American Indian tribes. Thus, Glooscap, culture hero of the Abnaki Indians of the Northeastern Woodlands, overcomes a giant bird whose wings cause the wind. He breaks one of the organs of aerial flight. When the wing heals, it is a great deal smaller, and when flapped, it produces light, gentle movements of air.

Almost all over the continent there exist origin stories of the establishment of the winds at the four quarters of the earth, and some Indian tribes envisage more than those of the four direc-

81

Boreas. The north wind is depicted as a winged, bearded man holding a conch shell. Insofar as the sculptures represent the general character of the weather which the several winds bring, the tower may be regarded as a very early form of weather forecast.

tions. There are as well, in western American Indian mythologies particularly, tales of conflicts between the north and south winds, and of the winds being kept in a bag. In California and southern Oregon narratives, there is a cave in which they are confined and from which they are released.

Today *wind* is the general term for air naturally in motion, with whatever degree of velocity or force. The vertical movement of air is relatively small, especially near the earth's surface. Therefore, the word is usually restricted to signify almost exclusively horizontal movements. *Breeze* is popularly applied to a light, gentle wind. Meteorologically, it is any wind having a speed of from 4 to 31 miles an hour and is customarily used with a qualifying adjective, as light breeze, strong breeze, and so on. *Gale* is generally applied to a strong and somewhat violent wind and, meteorologically, to one having a velocity of from 32 to 63 miles an hour. Meteorologists also use this term with a qualifying adjective. *Gust* and *blast* denote a sudden, brief increase in the speed of the wind. One speaks, for example, of a March blast.

When differences in atmospheric pressure develop over the earth's surface, air is set in motion. Winds, then, are the result of pressure differences, which in turn arise from basic irregularities in the heating of the air. They are named in accordance with the direction from which they blow: thus a wind coming from the northwest is termed a "northwest" wind.

The best place and time to hear the howl of the wind at its loudest—and to feel its spell to the fullest—is in an exposed country house on a bleak winter night when a gusty gale is blowing. As it sweeps by the chimneys and over the gables, the wind sounds like the loud, protracted mournful cry of a dog or a wolf. If one is alone and thinks of werewolves, the effect is quite frightening.

The howl is, however, not the voice of a man transformed into a wolf in appetite and form. It, like other aeolian sounds, is due to eddy motions in the atmosphere immediately beyond the obstructing agent. An *eddy* is a current of air running contrary to the main current, especially one moving circularly. Eddies occur on the side of an obstacle, such as a roof, opposite to that against which the wind blows. They tear loose from the

Varnum's headquarters. As the wind swept over the roof, James Mitchell Varnum heard it howling inside this tall, lean wintry-looking house. In 1777, the Revolutionary soldier was commissioned brigadier-general in the Continental army by General Washington and became active in recruitments and reenlistments.

Telephone poles. The humming of aerial wires—a pleasant sound—is loudest in winter time when the cold has pulled things taut. The tighter the wire becomes, the more rapidly the eddies produced there vary the tension on it. These variations of tension are transmitted to the poles, which, in turn, act as sounding boards, analogous to those of pianos, and, consequently, increase the volume of the hum, whatever its pitch.

roof and reform there with such frequency and regularity as to produce a more or less musical note. *Pitch* is controlled by the frequency with which eddies are formed and detached. Consequently, it rises and falls with the wind velocity.

The wild howl in the night is far louder inside the house than out. There one is far less disturbed by the many other outdoor noises, particularly the continuous *whisper of the wind* right in one's ears. This low, sibilant, rustling sound, as of whispered speech, is also an eddy effect. As might not be expected, the obstacle is the ear itself!

There have been many absurd explanations of the well-known humming of telephone and telegraph wires. As children apt to believe things on slight evidence, we were jokingly told that this phenomenon was caused by the messages in transit. Indeed, that explanation has been proposed in all seriousness. When the wind blows over the wires, they do give forth a low, murmuring indistinct sound, as from the blending of many voices.

However, the real explanation of the hum of wires is similar to that of the howl of the wind. Eddies form on the wire and produce a sound whose pitch is a function of wind speed and the thickness of the wire. Wire lines that sing are mounted on poles which are usually located along highways, railroads, and city streets.

Although many aeolian sounds are merely irregular noises, others involve fairly clear musical notes or humming sounds, like those just described. These are called *aeolian tones.*

9

Whisper of Trees, Murmur of the Forest, and Roar of the Mountain

Just as stretched wires produce aeolian tones, so do pine needles, bare twigs—small, slender branches without leaves—and even the branches of trees. Trees have voices. Moreover, they are characteristic of the species.

Have you ever heard the muffled plaint of the oak at the wintry blast? Because relatively large and of many sizes, the twigs and branches of the tree produce a multitude of low tones. This grumbling has little in common with the sibilant sigh of the pine. The fine needles of the pine tree give a smaller range of high-pitched notes. Both the oak and the pine are spread over north temperate regions, providing one with ample opportunity to hear them speak.

Each twig and other similar obstacle in the wind, then, produces an aeolian note. The question is, how do a great number of such notes blend together? To put this in another way, how are the pitch and loudness of the resulting sound related to the like properties of the constituents?

Branch tip of red pine. When your mood is just right and you are all alone in a secluded place, there is nothing more solemnly pleasing to the ear than the dirge of an old pine tree. A tree with long needles sings most effectively. The blend of all the aeolian tones produced by the needles, with the variations in loudness and pitch that occur with the ceaseless changes of the wind, make up the endless mournful song.

(OPPOSITE) *Swamp white oak without leaves.* The oak gruffly grumbles at a violent gust of winter wind. Each twig of this tree growing in Michigan feebly mumbles the one note it can, and must, as determined by its diameter and the speed of the moving air.

A multitude of sounds merge into a seeming note whose pitch is the approximate average of those of the many components. Hence, the *whisper of a tree* has substantially the same pitch as that of its individual twigs, or its needles, if the tree be a pine. Similarly, the hum of a swarm of bees is pitched to that of the average bee, and the concert of myriad mosquitoes is only the magnified whine of the type.

According to another law of sound, it can be stated that the mean intensity of a composite note is the sum of the individual intensities. Thus, though the note of the twig may be inaudible, even at close range, the tree may frequently be heard some distance away.

Just as the aeolian notes of the countless needles on a single pine tree, or the many twigs on an oak, blend into a whisper of the same average pitch but immensely greater volume, so, too, the whisperings of a large number of individual trees merge into the familiar *murmur of the forest*. Shelley, the English poet, speaks of "the breeze murmuring in the musical woods." Indeed, the whole forest makes a low, confused, and indistinct sound like a multitude of living creatures. This sound often can be heard a mile away—and sometimes much farther.

Conditions suitable for forest growth are found over very large areas of the earth's surface, and forest is the most extensive type of natural vegetation. But all over the world sounding woods have been cleared and silenced. In the United States, ruthless exploitation in 300 years has destroyed nearly half the area covered mainly with trees. If this destruction continues, the murmur of the forest may be only a memory to future generations of Americans, as well as to other peoples of the world.

Another example of the combined effects of myriads upon myriads of aeolian whispers is the *roar of the mountain*. A moun-

Ancient white oaks without leaves. Groves and forests have been murmuring ever since there were trees and winds to blow through them. Oaks are hardy and have a long life, up to 700 years or more. This group of trees on Gardiner's Island, New York, has been growing since colonial days— or before. How many generations have stopped by the wood and heard its murmur!

St. Joe National Forest. This dense growth of trees and underbrush is located in the rugged Bitterroot Range of the Idaho-Montana divide. The range, named for the bitterroot plant which is found there, is largely forested. Certain mountains such as these produce muffled roars in the valleys opposite to the direction from which the wind blows.

tain is a land mass rising conspicuously above its surroundings. These elevations are usually found connected in chains or ranges, with elongated depressions, or valleys, between them. When such a landform is well wooded along and near its top, and when it is crossed by a wind, one often hears a low sighing or moaning noise in the leeward valley. As the wind over the mountaintop grows to a gale, the noise gradually swells to a roar, as of a distant mighty cataract. The voice so aroused is roughly focused or concentrated by the descending wind upon the valley. The focusing admittedly greatly accentuates the effect, which is most striking and at times even awe-inspiring.

The best time of year to hear this noise is during winter, when there are no protecting leaves on the trees, or at any time if the forest is pine. The roar can be heard in mountainous regions throughout the world.

10

Shriek and Howl of
the Devil's Fiddle
and Rustle of Leaves

A strange kind of weather music is the *shriek and howl of the devil's fiddle*. Of these fiddles, there are many sizes and grades. One of the most effective is a tall, dead tree which has, in falling, caught in the fork of a nearby companion. The companion tree swinging from side to side in the wind has worn both, at their place of contact, down to the hard, dry wood beneath. Now the two trees move back and forth on each other as swayed by the wind, not smoothly, but in numerous

White-barked quaking aspen. The aspen is a tree characterized by its tremulous leaves. The design of the leafstalks—slender, flattened, and very flexible—allows the thin papery foliage to respond to the slightest air current. By their friction on each other, the leaves give rise to a rustling sound. The quaking or trembling aspen has the widest range of any American tree, being found from Labrador to the Yukon and south to Kentucky, and along mountain ranges to Mexico. It is common in all the Canadian provinces. The bark of the young tree is yellowish-green or nearly white, such as these trees lining a trail in Rocky Mountain National Park.

jerks, much as a resined bow moves across the strings of a violin. These sharp, suddenly arrested motions knock the air into corresponding sound waves, hardly capable of being heard when the wind is light but curdling shrieks when it is high and gusty.

The devil's fiddle is not known for beauty of tone and design. The sound it produces is always weird and startling. However, under the right conditions, the instrument is just as successful in arousing one's feelings as a Stradivarius. If you are alone at night in a forest when a storm is gathering, you will jump to this music of the Prince of Darkness.

The *rustle of leaves* can also be startling. The quick succession or confusion of small sounds is due to the rubbing together of the foliage as trees and branches or stalks of corn are shaken by the movement of air. The normal method of gathering the responses of a famous oracle at Dodona, an ancient town in northwest Greece, was by listening to sounds such as these.

Dodona stands on a windswept plateau just under Mount Tomarus in Epirus. This was the seat of a temple to Zeus and the oldest of the Greek oracles, or mediums by which deities were consulted. The responses of the oracle of Zeus were read in the rustling of the leaves of a sacred oak, or the murmuring of a spring which gushed from its roots. The sounds were interpreted by attendant priests and later priestesses of advanced age.

In the autumn, when dead leaves are driven roughly over

(OPPOSITE) *Windblown cornstalks.* The stalks with large but narrow leaves stand out against the sky on a blustery autumn day in Saratoga County, New York. The voice of Indian corn can be heard in the fields—a voice aroused by the wind.

Wood grass. Indian grass, as it is also called, has long flat leaves that are rough and raspy and produce a distinct sound when they rub against each other. One of the most important constituents of the North American prairie, the tall perennial grass bears narrow, greatly branched flower clusters, as this Kansas photograph shows. Each small, yellow spike is fringed with white hairs, giving the plant a silver-and-gold appearance.

the earth by the unseen presence of the wind, they move with
a harsher sound than the sacred language of rustling. Yellow,
and brown, and red, they skitter along the ground, fleeing like

Ruins of Dodona. This theatre, which underwent many changes, was constructed originally in the time of Pyrrhus, King of Epirus, who was born in 318 B.C. To the east of the theatre is the sacred precinct of Zeus, a complex ruin in which four stages of growth can be distinguished (at left in the picture but not shown). At first worship centered upon the oracular oak, which, according to Homer, was tended by priests with unwashed feet who slept on the ground; fragments of votive tripods of the eighth century B.C. have been recovered. A simple stone temple was not built until the fourth century B.C. This and the oak were then surrounded by a wall. The wall was replaced in the time of Pyrrhus by an enclosure of Ionic colonnades facing inwards on three sides with a blind wall on the east nearest the tree. After the burning of the sacred groves in 219 B.C., the temple was enlarged and the wall of the court was rebuilt with a monumental gateway. Luxuriant trees grow below the site today, but there are no oaks, except one planted by an archaeologist.

ghosts from an enchanter. Listen for this *scraping noise*—combined with rustling as the leaves rub against each other —in October.

Tornado. This noisy, violent whirling wind struck Enid, Oklahoma.

11

Roar of the Tornado and Song of the Sands

The smallest yet most fierce of all storms, the *tornado* is as noisy as it is destructive. It comes with unearthly *shrieks* in the sky and a deafening *roar* on the ground like that of passing freight trains.

The tornado, or *twister* as it is sometimes called, is a violently rotating column of air, hanging from the dark base of a cloud, and nearly always observable as a cloud in the shape of a funnel. It is commonly only several hundreds of yards in diameter, but the velocity of its upward-spiraling winds is estimated at 100 to more than 300 miles an hour!

The forward speed of this spectacular phenomenon is normally 30 to 40 miles an hour, and the length of its path is usually less than 25 miles. Its general direction of travel is determined by the motion of the parent cloud. Heavy rain and hail often accompany the tornado, as do thunder and lightning.

Where the tip of the funnel cloud touches the ground, great havoc is caused. Trees are uprooted, crops are flattened, and buildings are exploded to bits. In one case, a schoolhouse with 85 pupils inside was demolished and the children were carried 150 yards with none killed. In another, five railway coaches, each weighing 70 tons, were lifted from their track, and one coach was moved 80 feet.

Although much of the damage is done by winds, many of the phenomena are due to local pressure differences that occur as the tornado passes. No direct measurements have been made of pressures within a twister, but sudden drops have been recorded just outside the zone of destructive winds. These changes show that the normal force exerted by the air inside a building does not have time to adjust to the fast reduction outside, causing explosion or "suction" effects. Walls are blown outward and roofs are lifted upward.

The precise conditions required to produce a tornado are not clearly understood. Moreover, until more detail about the structure of a storm is known, all explanations of its acoustical properties must necessarily remain speculations. But the shrill, wild cries from above probably arise from turbulent eddies forming on the outward bounds of the whirl. By contrast, it has been reported that within the funnel of the tornado silence prevails. In some degree, the absolute stillness may be explained as a physiological result of the low external pressure on the ear and ensuing temporary impairment of the ability to hear. This may be combined with the effect of psychological shock on the part of the listener. The roar is undoubtedly due to the wreckage caused by the storm. And the more or less continuous rumble heard also is thunder.

Tornadoes occur on all continents, but nowhere are they as common as in the United States and Australia, where the average number is 140 to 150 each year. They strike through-

Aftermath of a tornado. The disastrous consequences of a storm in Missouri are plainly visible.

out the course of the four seasons and at any time of the day but are most frequent in spring and in middle and late afternoon.

In the United States, a vast *tornado belt* encompasses the great lowland areas of the central and upper Mississippi, the Ohio, and lower Missouri river valleys. This is the district of North America where you are most likely to see a commotion in a dark cloud which then spreads downward toward the earth in the shape of a cone, and to hear a roaring noise while the whirling pendant cloud is in touch with, or even closely approaches, the ground.

No work on meteorological acoustics would be complete without some account of the so-called *song of the sands*. Man's love of the marvelous and mysterious has been rewarded by the discovery at various places and points of time of accumulations of stone particles which make musical sounds.

Sand is a loose material composed of small but easily distinguishable grains, most commonly quartz, resulting from the disintegration of rocks. It consists of particles that range in diameters from about 0.002 to 0.08 inch and is much written about in fairy tales as the substance dusted in children's eyes to make them sleepy. The term sand, often used in the plural, also means a tract or area of sand. "Even as men wrecked upon a sand," writes the poet Shakespeare.

Sound-making sand is associated with sea and freshwater *beaches* and with high *dunes* and *sandbanks*. The golden grains accumulated along seashores and lakeshores are borne up by the waves and left between the lines of high and low water. In different parts of the world, these beaches *squeak* or *whistle* when walked over, struck by the foot, or stroked by the hand. In hills composed of or covered with sand, the little grains are

104

Musical sand. In July and August, 1884, Professor H. Carrington Bolton, Trinity College, Hartford, and Dr. Alexis A. Julien, Columbia College, New York, conducted experiments at the so-called "singing beach" at Manchester, Massachusetts. The character of the sounds obtained by friction on the beach was decidedly musical, and the investigators were able to indicate the exact notes on a musical staff. The shrillness and lowness of note depended chiefly on the quantity of the sand disturbed. By plunging both hands into the loose material and bringing them together quickly with a swoop, a large quantity of the small grains vibrated and they heard a tone of which the dominant note was:

By striking the sand nearer the surface and with less force, very high notes were perceived somewhat confused. The following were heard at different times:

By rubbing a double handful of the sand firmly and briskly, several notes on a rising scale were discerned, the notes rising as the quantity of material between the hands diminished. They did not hear each note of the scale separately, but the ear received an impression something like that formed by sliding a finger up a violin string at the same time the bow is drawn:

The range was very remarkable and decided. The sonorous sand of another beach, where Professor Bolton and Dr. Julien conducted experiments that same summer, gave somewhat different tones. At Far Rockaway, Long Island, the B below the staff was not heard at all. But the following notes were perceived at different times according to the manner of the friction:

In both cases, the notes were determined by comparison with those made on a violin at concert pitch.

---

piled up by the wind. It is these hills of windblown particles, whose steep slopes give rise to acoustic phenomena of great magnitude, that are of primary interest here.

Allusions to sonorous sands are scattered sparingly through the writings of more than a thousand years. *The Arabian Nights,* a collection of ancient tales from Arabia, Persia, India, and other lands, mentions them. Old Chinese chronicles tell of such a site in the desert of Lob Nor. Marco Polo, the Venetian traveler in eastern Asia, narrates superstitions concerning the phenomenon. Baber, founder and first emperor of the Mogul dynasty of India, refers to a singing sands locality of Afghanistan. And many travelers in the East give accounts of hills of moving sand which emit mysterious noises.

In the nineteenth century, a number of scientists described Gebel Nakous or the Mountain of the Bell. This famous mountain is situated near Tor, a town in the Sinai Peninsula in northeast Egypt, on the coast of Suez. It was reported that several large banks of sand rested on the steep slopes of this mountain, one of which emitted distinct musical sounds whenever the loose material slid down the incline either spontaneously or through the action of man. The sand was blown up on the mountainside by violent winds. When it accumulated in such quantity as to exceed the angle of rest, it slid down the incline. The movement was accompanied by a musical tone "resembling the lowest bass note of an organ with a tremolo stop." The Bedouins of the region accounted for the phenomenon by attributing it to the *nakous* or wooden gong of a subterranean monastery in the heart of the mountain. These desert dwellers claimed the sounds could only be heard at the hours of prayer.

A hill resembling the Mountain of the Bell exists near Kabul in Afghanistan. It is called Rege-Rawan or the Moving Sand and was described by Baber: "Between these plains there is a small hill in which there is a line of sandy ground, reaching from the top to the bottom of the hill. . . . They say that in summer the sound of drums and *nagarets* [kettle drums] issues from this sand." Those who ventured there in later years found Baber's description accurate. When the sand deposited by the wind was set in motion by a body of people, who slid down it, hollow sounds were heard such as would be made by a large drum.

The Rege-Rawan. Captain Alexander Burnes visited the vicinity of Kabul in October, 1837. A sheet of sand as pure as that on the seashore formed the face of the hill to its summit, which was 400 feet high. In this contemporary sketch, the sand is being set in motion by people sliding down the elevation, in order to disclose the curiosity.

The "barking sands" on the island of Kauai, Hawaii, are mentioned in the works of several sojourners. When moved, the material on the top and the landward slope of a particular dune possessed remarkable acoustic properties, likened to the bark of a dog. As sand dunes were commonly used for burial places, the native Hawaiians said the noise was due to the spirits of the dead, who grumbled at being disturbed. In Nevada, a similar phenomenon is described: a dune called Sand Mountain has often been heard to *boom*.

Booming dunes, which in some places startle the silence of

108

the desert, are well known. According to one reporter in south-
western Egypt, the vibrant deep hollow sound was so loud he
had to shout to be heard by his companion. Set going by the
disturbance, other sources joined their music to the first, with
so close a note that a slow beat was discerned. This weird
chorus continued on a still night for several minutes before

Sahara's swelling dunes. Rippled by the wind and stamped with men's
and camel's footprints, these dunes are located in a vast region of deserts
and oases in North Africa. Camels and gowned Moslems perch on the
ocean of sand amid long shadows at dusk. Do they hear the sounds produced by desert dunes? Some say that standing on the sand when it is
singing is like resting on a huge stringed instrument while a bow is being
drawn slowly across it.

silence was restored and the ground ceased to tremble.

It has been discovered that the grains of sand that sing are polished, free from fragments, and nearly all within a certain narrow range of size. Scientists generally agree that the sounds are caused by the rubbing of these grains against each other. But as yet there is no real explanation of the mechanism by which they are produced.

When you are in the desert, listen for the song of the sands— one of the strangest musical performances in nature.

Afterword

In addition to the foregoing meteorological sounds, there are others whose explanations are easy, if not immediately obvious, such as the *tap of branches*. Consider the wisteria. These twining woody vines or shrubs have fruits that are elongated pods and showy clusters of bluish, white, pink, or purplish flowers. Native to the eastern United States and eastern Asia, they attach themselves to and climb on supporting structures. In New York City, one of these handsome leguminous plants has fastened itself to two ropes and climbed five stories toward the light, covering the brownstone façade of my townhouse.

In the winter, when the compound leaves have fallen off the vine, and when the house is swept by winds, I hear a tap, tap, tap at the window. It sounds like a tired man is tapping at the glass with his hand, trying to get my attention, but no one is there. Or rather it is only the woody claws growing from the main stem of the wisteria striking the window with slight audible blows. In the country, branches of trees close to houses often knock at windows—just another effect of the wind.

At the shore, there is no end of still another acoustical

phenomenon, the widely known *roar of waves*. These ridges on the surface of the sea have normally a forward motion and are caused, for the most part, by wind. It is their breaking into foam against the shore that produces the voice of the vast waters. As

the land bordering the sea is extensive, there is abundant opportunity to listen to what the wild waves are saying. Sometimes I hear this roar all day long in a house on an island in southeastern New York, between Great South Bay and the Atlantic.

Breaking waves. Their foam, splash, and sound are familiar to those living on the land bordering the sea, as on the Atlantic coast photographed here.

113

Hurricane. Few people fail to be stirred by the ominous pounding of the *surf* as a hurricane approaches. When the storm arrives, the shrieking and roaring of the wind, exceeding 75 miles an hour, the beating of torrential rain, and the cracking of nearby thunder combine to form one of the great symphonies of nature. Such a "composition" was produced in September, 1945, at Bayfront Park, Miami.

The house stands in a miniature forest of holly, pitch pine, black gum, red oak, and sassafras—whose murmur often merges into a mighty chorus with the sea. How many more of these common meteorological sounds can you name?

For those who desire to continue their study of atmospheric acoustics, there are a number of other noises to consider that are usually included under this subject. There are the *det-*

onations of meteors, rare events confined to definite places. *Meteors* are fragments of iron or stone that enter the earth's atmosphere from outer space and are there made to glow with intense heat caused by compression of air in front of the particles. Some of these objects, *fireballs,* are bright enough to light up the landscape and to cast shadows on the ground. When a very large ball of fire traverses the sky, the sound produced is frequently startling, like the thundering of guns. These detonations give evidence of the arrival of shock waves and the sound of air collapsing into the semivacuum created along the curve described by the fiery mass. A portion of the object may fall to earth as a *meteorite.*

In many cases, *whistling, whining,* or *hissing noises* have been heard at the same time the fireball was sighted or have drawn the observer's attention to it, the typical explosion being heard after some minutes. It has been proposed that they are electrical in origin and are caused by the mass of air converted into electrified particles by collision with the fireball. But these noises have not been fully explained. From their arrival time, they cannot be normal sound waves.

There are *brontides,* low rumbling, thunderlike noises of short duration that have been heard in ancient and modern times in various parts of the world. Often occurring when the sky is clear, they seem to come from a distance, but are of uncertain direction, and are most frequent in regions where earthquakes are active. In numerous instances, the noises occurred at irregular intervals over a period of months or years in a particular region, where they were given a local name. Thus, they are called Barisal guns in the Ganges Delta, *mistpoeffers* ("fog belchers") off the coast of Belgium, *brontidi* ("like thunder") in the Apennines, and Seneca guns in central New York State.

Earthquake damage. In March, 1964, considerable havoc was caused by the shaking of the earth in Alaska. Brontides have been well documented, often in association with seismic activity and in several cases as precursors to major earthquakes.

(OPPOSITE) *Fall of a fireball.* The awe-inspiring noise and lights accompanying some meteoric falls convinced men of ancient times that meteorites came from the gods; accordingly, they were venerated. This large ball of fire crossed the field of the camera while the spiral nebula in Andromeda was being photographed on September 12, 1923, at the Prague Observatory in Czechoslovakia. The galaxy of stars in Andromeda is seen at center, the great meteor below.

It appears that a noticeable sound may be generated by earth tremors that are too weak to be felt. This can account for many of these episodes but not all. Other causes related to seismic activity, such as the sudden eruption of gas from high-pressure sources in the ground, may at times have been responsible. And some of these noises may have been due to abnormal propagation of far-off thunder or artillery fire. Under certain atmospheric conditions, sounds can be heard at distances greater than 60 miles from their source, leaving an intervening shadow zone of silence.

In recent years, brontides have not been discussed much. Because of the greatly increased frequency of artificial explosive noises, they may not have been recognized as sounds of natural origin. But in light of the knowledge that they exist and that they have a possible relationship to earthquakes, the occurrence anywhere of mysterious episodes of thunderlike noises should be investigated. For the curious scientist beginning his career, there are many unsolved problems in the field of meteorological acoustics to explore.

Acknowledgments

Grateful acknowledgment is made to the following individuals, institutions, and publishers that have given permission for the use of illustrations:

American Airlines, Dallas, Texas, page 64

American Museum of Natural History, New York, N.Y., pages 74, 91, 116

Bell Laboratories, Murray Hill, N.J., page 85

British Museum, London, England, page 35

Greek National Tourist Organization, New York, N.Y., pages 98–99

National Aeronautics and Space Administration, Washington, D.C., page 22

National Center for Atmospheric Research, Boulder, Colorado, pages 24, 25, 48, 55, 62, 63, 100, 103

National Oceanic and Atmospheric Administration, Rockville, Maryland, pages 20, 46, 58–59, 80 (Ralph F. Kresge), 82 (Ralph F. Kresge), 112–113, 114, 117

National Park Service, Washington, D.C., pages 94, 97 (above)

The New York Public Library, Picture Collection, New York, N.Y., pages 28, 30, 31, 33, 40, 43, 69, 70, 84, 109

Society for the Preservation of New England Antiquities, Boston, Massachusetts, page 77

Swiss National Tourist Office, New York, N.Y., pages 66, 71, 72

U.S. Forest Service, Washington, D.C., frontispiece and pages 88, 89, 92

U.S. Geological Survey, Denver, Colorado, pages 52 (G. K. Gilbert), 53 (N. K. Huber)

U.S. Navy, Washington, D.C., page 51

The Washington Post, Washington, D.C., endpaper

Wide World Photos, New York, N.Y., page 97 (below)

The pictures on pages 105 and 106 are from "Musical Sand, Its Wide Distribution and Properties" by H. Carrington Bolton and Alexis A. Julien, *Proceedings of the American Association for the Advancement of Science,* vol. 33, Salem, 1884. The picture on page 108 is from "On the Reg-Ruwan or Moving Sand, a Singular Phenomenon of Sound near Cabúl with a Sketch" by Alex Burnes, plate 18, *The Journal of the Asiatic Society of Bengal,* vol. 7, Calcutta, 1838. The picture on page 39 is from *L'Atmosphere, Description Des Grandes Phénomenes De La Nature* by Camille Flammarion, Deuxième Édition, Libraire Hachette Et Cie, Paris, 1873. The picture on page 38 is from *Eclairs et Tonnerre* by W. de Fonvielle, Deuxième Édition, Libraire Hachette Et Cie, Paris, 1869. The picture on page 16 is from *Travels in the Air* by James Glaisher, Camille Flammarion, W. de Fonvielle, and Gaston Tissandier, 2nd ed. revised, Richard Bentley & Son, London, 1871.

Annotated Bibliography

A list of the main sources of information on atmospheric acoustics and mythology used in the preparation of this book follows:

Bagnold, R. A. *The Physics of Blown Sand and Desert Dunes*. London: Methuen & Co. Ltd., 1941.
    A comprehensive work on the behavior of dry sand.

Humphreys, W. J. *Physics of the Air*. 3rd ed. revised. New York and London: McGraw-Hill Book Company, Inc., 1940.
    An orderly assemblage of the facts and theories of the numerous and important physical phenomena of the earth's atmosphere.

————. *Ways of the Weather: A Cultural Survey of Meteorology*. Lancaster: The Jaques Cattell Press, 1942.
    An attempt to correct the lack of knowledge which prevails about the commonest of all topics, the weather.

Leach, Maria (ed.) *The Standard Dictionary of Folklore, Mythology, and Legend*. New York: Funk & Wagnalls Company, 1949.
    A cross section of the spiritual content of the world, bringing together material heretofore scattered in journals, books, manuscripts, etc.

Neuberger, Hans. *Introduction to Physical Meteorology*. 2nd print. revised. University Park: Mineral Industries Extension Services, 1957.

A book based on a course in physical meteorology offered at The Pennsylvania State University for many years.

In addition to these books, articles in journals and magazines were consulted on specific phenomena, including:

Bolton, H. Carrington. "The 'Barking Sands' of the Hawaiian Islands." *Science* 16 (1890): 163–164.

————. "Researches on Sonorous Sand in the Peninsula of Sinai." *Proceedings of the American Association for the Advancement of Science* 38 (1889): 137–140.

Bolton, H. Carrington, and Julien, Alexis A. "Musical Sand, Its Wide Distribution and Properties." *Proceedings of the American Association for the Advancement of Science* 33 (1884): 408–413.

Burnes, Alex. "On the Reg-Ruwan or Moving Sand, a Singular Phenomenon of Sound near Cabúl with a Sketch." *The Journal of the Asiatic Society of Bengal* 7 (1838): 324–325.

Gold, Thomas, and Soter, Steven. "Brontides: Natural Explosive Noises." *Science* 204 (1979): 371–374.

Sverdrup, H. U. "Audibility of the Aurora Polaris." *Nature* 128 (1931): 457.

Index

About the Author

KENNETH HEUER, educator, writer, and publishing company executive, began his career as lecturer and teacher of astronomy at the American Museum-Hayden Planetarium in New York. Later he entered the publishing field and was director of the science book departments of several publishers, as well as a vice president. He is currently New York editor of a leading university press.

His books include *Men of Other Planets, The Next Fifty Billion Years, An Adventure in Astronomy,* and *City of the Stargazers.* His most recent work, *Rainbows, Halos, and Other Wonders,* was named an Outstanding Science Trade Book for Children by the National Science Teachers Association-Children's Book Council Joint Committee. He has also contributed articles and book reviews to national magazines and newspapers.

A fellow of the Royal Astronomical Society, member of the Explorers Club, and an associate benefactor of the American Museum of Natural History, Mr. Heuer lives in New York City.